CONTENDER
OF
CHAOS

poems by

Laureen Summers

Finishing Line Press
Georgetown, Kentucky

CONTENDER OF CHAOS

Copyright © 2020 by Laureen Summers
ISBN 978-1-64662-155-2 First Edition
All rights reserved under International and Pan-American Copyright Conventions. No part of this book may be reproduced in any manner whatsoever without written permission from the publisher, except in the case of brief quotations embodied in critical articles and reviews.

ACKNOWLEDGMENTS

My deep appreciation to Anne Becker for working with and encouraging me to produce this chapbook. Thanks also to the Writing A Village poetry workshop in Takoma Park, Maryland.

Publisher: Leah Maines
Editor: Christen Kincaid
Cover Art: Jackie L. Braitman, http://jackiebraitman.com
Author Photo: Roy E. Zimmerman
Cover Design: Elizabeth Maines McCleavy

Printed in the USA on acid-free paper.
Order online: www.finishinglinepress.com
　　　　　　also available on amazon.com

　　　　　　　Author inquiries and mail orders:
　　　　　　　　　Finishing Line Press
　　　　　　　　　　P. O. Box 1626
　　　　　　　　Georgetown, Kentucky 40324
　　　　　　　　　　　U. S. A.

Table of Contents

This is About a Body 1

Prelude 2

Birth and Other Vignettes 3

The Scent on Her Pillow 7

They Would Never Call it a Suicide 8

I Refuse to be a Wallflower with You 9

Fireflies 10

Sunrise in July 11

The Boy in the Window 12

The Woman on the Train 13

Ode to Kelsey 15

Reflection of A December Day 16

One Saturday Morning 17

The Woman in Purple 18

Vacation in Maine 19

DuPont Circle 21

When I was 66 22

Re-Creation 23

Fire at Night 24

Our Neighbors 25

The Reading 26

The Daughter of My Heart 27

For Sheldon 28

My First Real Love Poem 29

Hurricane Irene 30

*To my husband Earl Shoop
and daughter Melanie Zimmerman*

THIS IS ABOUT A BODY

that moves with desire.
It's about a body wanting more
than everything—a body to which
some would turn away
from its uncoordinated movements
and slurry speech.

Please don't call this body
Courageous
Or inspirational
Or brave
But consider how this body felt when
a thousand dreams came true.

If you doubt that this body
can hike through leaf-laden woods;
dance to boisterous songs;
or practice aerobics in a swimming pool,
listen to the reason of those who
tested out their assumptions,
then began to change their minds.

Sometimes this body asks for help
on stairs with no railings; during receptions
when food is carefully balanced and drink
is easy to spill; on forms where writing
challenges anyone. But still—
this body deserves everything…a body
living in the unthinkable moments of time.

PRELUDE—Cazenovia 1965-67

Cazenovia—a town bordered by a lake where
autumn leaves fall and lie lightly…where evening
shadows stretch long—and reminds one of the passing time.

Cazenovia—a college nourishing women's
dreams—where classes spoke to
inspiring minds—a town of stately homes and
friendly shopkeepers…where week-end soirees and
dates with men were reminders that we
were not alone.

Walks along the lake became a passion…
an escape from expectant professors
and afternoon teas. Yet, the constant greetings
 upon my return were reassuring, even when
we were all hurrying somewhere.

1965 was the year of the east coast black-out and
 the biggest snowstorm. Bursts of laughter
ruptured the dark as we gathered in candle-lit dorms
wondering if our studies promised success
and our friendships would last forever.

The lake provided solace whenever I felt afraid.
The trees, bending across the waters beckoned.
I was the naked, young willow weeping for maturity….
perhaps the next blossoming
had already begun.

BIRTH AND OTHER VIGNETTES

I

They met through a war correspondence
and married in her house in the Bronx.
They lived in an apartment in Greenwich Village
with a garden of flowers in the back.

She was sick in her seventh month
of pregnancy. Phlebitis in her leg.
He forbid an operation.
It might leave a scar.

I was born not breathing; given oxygen too late to
prevent brain damage; and was separated from my mom
for five days.

There were no details.

II.

"She can't hold her head up," my grandmother said, "she drools."
"It will go away" my father replied.
"She has cerebral palsy," a cousin-doctor said.
"Oh no!" my mother cried.

But she always told me I was loved.

III.

My father played with me at the beach and took me walking
on Sundays. There were monkeys in the shoe store window
downtown and turtles in the woods.
"She's a fighter," he said.

My dad had a great sense of adventure.
He didn't love many people, but I think he loved me.

IV.

My brother was born when I was 7. He was a perfect infant
who never cried. His nurse had drugged him to keep him calm.
Now, a mathematical genius who makes people smile,
he has no room for emotional turmoil.

He is my hero.

V.

When I was 10, we moved to Puerto Rico.
I took long walks around our neighborhood.

One day, a man followed me home in his car.
      "Do you know where she's been?" he asked.
          "You should keep her inside."

My mother smiled and I kept on walking.

VI.

In high school, the dating-mating game
      did not invite me to play.
Classmates said I was a nice person—generous and kind.

The boys took turns dancing with me
at all the parties.

The girls shared their secrets.

But—I wanted to hear that I was beautiful;
I wanted men to whistle and follow me with their eyes—all the
uncomfortable advances most young women hate.

I wanted everything I thought I couldn't have.

VII.

I went to the senior prom with a brilliant boy from Cuba.
We used to argue in Philosophy class. Our friends helped him
choose a jacket and he brought me a corsage. I wore a long dress
with embroidered daisies. We danced and talked until early in the
morning.

He is still my friend.

VIII.

In college, I studied Liberal Arts. I attended four schools
in five years. I worked at unsatisfying jobs until I
found a career in science—a subject I was never good at.

IX.

I learned to weave and was able to manipulate
a warp and a weft. My first project was a wall hanging
in white. Simple designs, texture, and color defined
my many pieces.

When I could afford it, I bought every kind of yarn
and felt like an artist.

X.

My doctor told me my muscles are fine.
It is the messages from the brain that confuses
their movements.
I do not like the reactions from strangers.
I have no patience for myself.
I still don't understand my birth.
I question why I cannot appreciate the great life I lead.

It's not just my muscles that are confused.

THE SCENT BENEATH HER PILLOW

My mother liked music and art and gourmet meals;
She could play the violin and was an admirer of fine fashion.
She thought people who traveled were the most interesting
and that blondes had more fun.

She married my father in rebellion
to a lifestyle and a religion she did not understand, then
blamed him for all his trespasses.
She believed in Sigmund Freud and poker.
My brother was her golden child.

And then, there was me.

Does anyone want a disabled child? She made sure
I was treated like anybody else. She taught in the
neighborhood school so I could attend and
was proud of how I "overcame" my disability.
As adults we argued over ideas, friends, and
how I managed money. I tried to please her.
But everything that seemed right
                  always turned out wrong.

At age 91 She could not bear the loss of independence
or her body's need for intervention.
"You are nothing without love," she once said.
She could not tell how much we loved her.

In the fall, she made a decision.

Afterwards, I sat beside her until they came to take her away.
We made the arrangements; packed her things;
and paid her bills. I slept wrapped in her sheets
                  and caressed the scent of her beneath her pillow.

THEY WOULD NEVER CALL IT A SUICIDE

At 6 months he was a charmer
precocious, handsome and already
painfully shy.
He wouldn't respond to anyone but her.

At 1 year, he reached out his arms
only to be brushed aside
by the rustle of her skirts
as she moved, frantically, against the day.

At 2 years, he slept restlessly—
desperate in his dreaming.
His tears filled his face
and sealed the loneliness around his eyes.

At 3 years, he could not ask the question—
But he already knew the answer.

At the beach that summer, he played alone.
One afternoon he wandered away
knowing he should never leave without her.
But—the day was beautiful,
the sounds of the sea so gentle.

I REFUSED TO BE A WALLFLOWER WITH YOU
(For KEN COHEN—1968)

You appeared as the dance was beginning…
In the days when I looked for my life
And watched it move in ways I did not understand.
You were looking for a partner—
And for a little while,
I thought I wanted you.

We talked for hours—I listened
to your words—defiant and lonely.
Your eyes begged me to understand.
I waited for you to touch me—
But you kept your hands to yourself.

We went for drives—stopping at the top
of ski slopes where you hinted that we belonged
together.
    "Take me to your heart," you said,
    "Let us become one."

You wanted more than I was ever ready
to give.

I held on to a dream
Until you smashed it with your sorrow.
I wanted us to dance,
but you couldn't hear the music.

FIREFLIES

They come in the evening
when the day wants to curl around
the sun just one more time.
Their twinkle of lights leaves
invisible markings on the grass.

The lightning bugs, courting each other
on a warm summer evening, their mating calls
flicker back and forth chasing each other through the darkness.

The fireflies
come calling on a summer's evening
    without cell phones,
        or laptops,
            or the Sunday funnies…

I reach to touch their bodies as swiftly they pass me by.
    I wait for them to mate.

We all have mischief in our eyes.

SUNRISE IN JULY

This morning I burnt my hand on the toaster
in my eagerness for breakfast
and the sunrise on the beach.
My bathing suit had a tear
but I didn't care as morning breezes
followed my stroll along the ocean's edge.

A woman doing Yoga by the sand dunes
finished her routine. She called out
that yoga would be good for me and
assumed she understood a body she had never seen before.

A man fishing out to sea warned me
not to step on his fragile pole lines.
I walked cautiously behind him and hoped
he would haul in a catch to keep the sparkle in his eyes.

The beach warmed as a family staked their claim
on the still-moist sand.
Their children built sand castles around my feet.

It was time to go.

My feet tangled with the last waves
as the sea moved outward
and I moved inward.
I waved to the family; bowed to the fisherman;
winked at the Yoga lady
and turned towards home

THE BOY IN THE WINDOW

A paisley-colored shirt
spread over short brown pants...
He entered the window,
jumped down from the ledge
and walked across the room.

Was it just my imagination
that made me believe
an impossibility in the middle of the night?
I was three and still remember
the silence of his footsteps.

He was so small as he tiptoed
towards my parent's bed,
and cupped his hand close
to whisper into my father's ear.

He stood to walk back across the room.
Looking straight ahead and passing me by,
he climbed up the wall, and out the window.
My body quivered as I watched him leave.
       I still wait for his return.

THE WOMAN ON THE TRAIN

I.

The woman on the metro is putting
on her makeup, oblivious to any other rider.
Perhaps she wants to impress someone
waiting for her important contribution.

She opens her make-up case.
The person next to her raises his eyebrows
as she steadies her mascara brush and smears
her face with a lipstick-stained powder puff.

I don't understand putting on makeup in public.

II.

When I go home, left over concrete oozes out
from the rug covering our front steps; I'm afraid
of tripping. Inside, the workers leave paint globs
in selected corners of the room. We cover stained walls
with pictures and paintings.

Our kitchen is small with a broken
dishwasher and the ice maker is stuffed with a sock.
The vents are stuck closed against the warmth.
The workers smile at me and walk out the door.

For this, we pay ridiculous rent and try not to complain.

III.

Sometimes we shop at Whole Foods. Nobody looks
very happy. I would think they would be excited
by spending more money than they have.
I smile as I find more and more exotic foods
to test the boundaries of my credit card.

At the check-out, the cashiers don't look happy, either.
My husband likes to make them laugh—a bit of
reassurance that someone notices and actually
wants them to have a nice day.

All I want to do is go home and eat.

IV.

People on the train rush to give me their seat.
I admit I'm grateful.
Sometimes I think that
watching me walk in strange contortions
is probably interesting to someone who
                moves perfectly fine.

Bodies that move tell stories. I insist
on dancing even with the pain. I hide my secrets
amidst the varicose veins of my mind.

I keep trying to redefine exactly who I am. Sometimes
I really wonder. Maybe I should put on more make-up;
be another lady on the train.

ODE TO KELSEY

Her eyes pierce the morning—my grand-daughter.
She is impatient to start the day.
At 16 Months
She understands everything and responds
with her very own sounds.

We read books.
She loves books –
Never tiring of opening one
And then reaching for another
Until her room is filled with words.

We play together—
toys that talk and bounce and sing
She dumps puzzles and blocks
that slide across the floor.
We dance to songs and our bodies
       move casually together.

We go to the park—She laughs at my clumsiness
For once, I don't mind.
She watches the world from a swing,
and discovers the sandbox,
where she shares her toys.

In the evening
She bathes in colored bubbles
then crawls inside her mother's arms.
They share a story; a cuddle; a song.
She reluctantly puts away the day
and waits for the light of morning.

REFLECTIONS OF A DECEMBER DAY

My daughter was there –
Full of life
waiting for the results of my surgery
while sitting beside her dad.

A family was in the room
and they shared stories and pictures—
laughing.
Strangers in a room of expectations.
The calm before the storm.

She was a witness—
to the constant updates—and the family's movement to a private corner of the room.
"It can't be good," my daughter said.
A tragedy impossible to bear
when a wife and mother died…
A leak that wouldn't stop,
and a tired heart did not allow time to say good-bye.

My daughter held another daughter for a long, long time.

Fragile lives hang in balance
between healing and despair.

    Driving home, her hand was on my shoulder.

ONE SATURDAY MORNING
March 2002

We met one Saturday morning.
You turned to walk beside me.
The sun had just risen and a deer crossed our path.
Talking was easy, but I didn't pay attention.
And I didn't look for you again.

A month later, you made sure
I noticed. Kind-hearted woman with rarely
an angry word. I wanted nothing
but to stay beside you forever.

You welcomed my visits and showed me
your work, your home, and the places
you liked to shop. We bought root beer floats.
I played with your foster son.
We spent hours together, sometimes sleeping
beside each other. But I understood
our feelings were not the same.

In time you married the love of your life.
I cheered you on and went home to mine.
Some days still fill with your voice.

    I would like to find you on another Saturday morning.

THE WOMAN IN PURPLE

She wears purple with pride.
My friend was the first passenger
when I learned to drive. She tried to
teach me how to cook. She appreciates
my sense of humor and my wild
imagination. I like her growing air
of self-confidence.

Purple hair, purple clothes, Her
bathroom is purple with the towels
I bought her in secret delight. Purple
makes us feel elegant as we stroll
together talking of husbands and children
and the politics of the day.

We reassure each other in the toughest of times.

My friend lives in a cozy house in a comfortable town.
She can walk to shops and restaurants and
the Sunday market. At night the streetlamps
make a haven when I drive away.
Sometimes the air is dark and you can see
the stars.

VACATION IN MAINE

7:00—I wake to cloudy skies in Maine and stare
at the pictures on the walls of our road-side motel.
The early morning is refreshing before a day of constant chatter.

7:30—my friend opens her eyes
and conversation begins.
"I have to fill the silence," she often tells
me. We get ready for the day and pack up the car.

9:00—We breakfast at the Maine Diner in Wells.
I have lobster quiche with a blueberry muffin.
She has eggs with cod fish cakes.

Both selections come with fruit.

10:00—The wind picks up as we explore the coast.
We walk the Marginal Way in Ogunquit.
                We eat too-expensive lobster overlooking
                            a parking lot.
                We go to LL Bean and don't buy anything.

11:00—We continue up the coast, stopping at beaches
with big rocks and pounding waves. The sand is crusty
beneath our feet. We collect shells and look for
seagulls.

12:00—Then they appear almost out of nowhere,
seeming to spill across the sky… We are quiet then—
not wanting our words to compete
with the magic of the day.

1:00—At a beach in York, people are collecting shells.
We lunch on salami and cheese with crisp crackers;
packages of nuts and fruit and dark chocolate. We drive
to a light house and take more pictures.

3:00—It's time to leave.
We are so glad to be together
        when the ocean roared with our laughter
                and the seagulls crossed the sun.

FIRE AT NIGHT

You sitting there
feet stretched out, arms bent upon one another
staring into a fire
that took so long in making.

Your eyes are serious
I wonder what touches your mind
Questions seeking answers
between the flames.

Your smiles are sad
and words lie unsaid.
The fire's crackle
is our conversation.

Later,
a burnt-out flame
me sitting near
an empty chair.

RE-CREATION

They say God created the world in seven days.

I reached into a dream
wrapped around a rainbow.
                of fading colors.

I walked beside the night
seeking comfort among the stars –
and looked up to see the man
                in the moon.

He stepped down
to stand inside my life
and watch my desperate moves.

"Is this what you want?" he asked.
"This is what I understand," I said.
      "You're a fool."
      "I know."
He shook his head.

He watched me stumble through my sadness.
then slowly beckoned,
            "I will not hurt you."
I moved into his arms and cried for seven days.

My tears became new-found hope.
We talked for a long time.
            "Your life will be different, now," he said.
He climbed up to his place inside the moon.

I reached into a dream
            and pulled out my happiness.
The colors of the rainbow were brilliant
            and I was free.

…and on the last day, God created woman
            and gave her the power to change the world.

WHEN I WAS 66

In my 66th year –
Mary Kay taught me about make-up.
I wanted a pretty face.
All I needed was a cleanser,
moisturizer, and a good foundation.
I liked to add a little blush.

I wore clothes that spoke in colors –
Warm and radiant, they took me through
the long winter when the sky was full of snow
and the cold tried to wrap around my bones.

At 66, I subscribed to the New Yorker
and got hooked on British TV.
I walked in the woods on Sundays
and went in search of nourishing conversation.
My friends loosened their dreams
while I tightened the hold on mine.

I bought yarns, and wove on my loom for hours;
went Zumba dancing; and tried to make my home a place of beauty.
My husband and I decided we were still in love.
Our roller-coaster marriage defined us and
after 38 years, I took him off probation.

When I was 66, my grandson was born
with a hole in his diaphragm and fluid in his chest.
He had a ventilator, feeding tubes, drugs, tests and surgery –
He never doubted his will to live
or the parents who healed him with their love.

Bodies forever challenge us.
I look at my own—
Different in so many ways
People often hesitate…
But this body is all I have and at 66, it still belongs to me.

DUPONT CIRCLE—1973

I
Washington D.C. sizzles in the heat
as artists and revolutionaries peddle their dreams
and the street people look for answers to their loneliness
amidst hand-me-down quarters and left-over dimes.

II
In a corner café on R street, the intellectuals
gather, their conversations urgent
as they order tea and croissants and find comfort
among those who agree with their every word.

III
In a bookstore on P Street, the poets read their poems,
snap their fingers when a verse resonates
with the story of their lives.

IV
In DuPont Circle—the men playing chess games reflect
an energy that has onlookers mesmerized. Passersby
walk by the center fountain and scream in delighted
protest as the water spray touch their outstretched arms.

V
On 19th and 20th streets, the residents are lesbian and gay and black
and brown and disabled and straight and female and everyone
tries not to blame everyone else for everything that has ever gone
wrong. Perhaps the essence of their lives will not be forgotten.

VI
It is early summer and the sunsets take their time.
Every night seems shorter than yesterday.
People, from everywhere, draw close and would-be lover's hands
slip inside each other when no one is looking.

OUR NEIGHBORS

The man next door smokes on his porch, watching a hawk
nesting in a tree across the street. He works for friends and
is expert at building and repairing almost anything.
He likes to admonish me when I'm rushing off to some meeting.

"You'll never make it in time," he says as I race my car out of the
driveway.

In the summer, his girlfriend and I go to the Sunday Market. She
helps me climb into her truck and makes sure I bring my 'handicapped'
placard—we have a special parking spot that's usually empty. She likes
to look at everything and we return home with plants and flowers
we never meant to buy.

She used to work in a print shop; then at the Senior Center
down the street. I like her down-to-earthiness and
love of simple things. She grew up in the house next door
and brings us homemade food and sweet companionship.

They go to his family's home in the country. She likes to cook
for his brothers in return for a night of fresh air and silence. He
only wants to be with her.

Once, he danced with me—the time we all went out to eat—
in celebration of their generosity when we moved into our house
and they had helped us—hardly knowing who we were.

Sometimes in the evenings, we sit outside and roast marshmallows.
In the mornings, I look out of my windows to wave. Their home
Is full of knick-knacks and neater than mine will ever be.
I find solace every time I see their truck in the driveway.
                    I want to be let in.

THE READING

At first, he looked disheveled…
a tall man in a paisley-printed shirt
not quite tucked into his pants. I could almost
hear his thoughts—"will the audience like me?"

His voice was steady and, when he read from his book,
his words were music—the notes were strong and deep.

 He wrote about wars and the people who lived inside his head.
He talked about relationships and knew that being brave
was never good enough for a lonely man.

He spoke about a life—the moments of joy …

the night so long ago

when his baby girl threw up in his face and he held her
as they showered together; then tucked her
tenderly back to sleep.

 He told about

the days of tension between him and his son
until his son came to his bedroom, "Dad, I have to tell you
something—I'm gay." and the incredible relief that filled up
both.

At first, he looked disheveled. And then he spoke his mind.

THE DAUGHTER OF MY HEART

A shock of black hair emerged as my doctor helped her birth.
She was perfect and beautiful. I could hardly believe
she was mine.

We brought her home dressed in lavender.

I wouldn't stop holding her,
letting her sleep on my chest,
in my bed, and everywhere else but her crib.

I told her about my disability early in her life,
and apologized for my awkward movements.
She relied on me for comfort, but, out in the world,
 she stayed close by her father's side.

Swimming and softball
        Ballet and gymnastics
                Car trips and camping
                        Playgrounds and parties

I wanted to give her everything.

College took her to the other side of the state and I cried.
It felt unbearable to let her go.

My daughter married a man who loved her. Her children mimic
her strength, her love and her confidence.

The teacher in her reaches out to me
when I get that wide-eyed look of frustration.
Then someone tells a joke and we both dissolve
into fits of relief and laughter.

She is the daughter of my heart.

FOR SHELDON

A breeze moves the ducktail curl
at the back of your neck
and you do that twitching thing with your shoulders
as I hurry to catch up with you.
A smile lights your face as you think of the next teaser
that will make me laugh.

Seven years younger, you relied on me for comfort
when we were small and you crawled into my bed.
You would fall asleep as I listened to the sounds
of our parent's unhappiness, wishing
they would find some peace
and give us back our childhoods.

The years filled with our busyness –
You chose a life of numbers;
I chose a life of words.
We married those we loved
and built our families carefully.

Two roads diverged……
I read Robert Frost while Daddy lay dying.
He squeezed my hand.
You arrived late,
but Mom needed you more.

3,000 miles apart.
You make fun of my seriousness;
I embrace your refusal to reassure.
We stay connected by months of soft silence.

Then, you call unexpectedly:
"I'm in town—Let's get together later".
I drop my life; unplan the day.
You have always made the difference
and I can barely wait to see you.

MY FIRST REAL LOVE POEM

His eyes meet mine
        as we walk the forest floor.
We look for tree doors—
the openings at the base of a trunk.

There was love when we married in the Spring.
I climbed a hill in the country surrounded
by wildflowers, good friends and 100 extension cords
running up the hill from a house a quarter mile away.

We knew our life together would not be easy but
we would understand
that our differences could never tear us apart.

There is love when the moon swells against the sky;
When I can't sleep—and I call for him to come…
His arms wrap around my body
and I rest contented.

There is love when the fire of our words
matches the passion in our hearts.
We remember the goodness of our lives
                and the sweet tenderness
of wanting each other.

HURRICANE IRENE
(In 2011, Hurricane Irene threatened destruction in her voyage up the east coast which included Washington, DC)

Irene came up the coast—contender of chaos...
A voluptuous female disrupting
routine lives and busy minds.

People clinging to normalcy could
barely stand the storm.

It was the anticipation that excited me;
The urgency for bottled water;
More food
         than
                 ever
                         before—

Chests of ice and colored candles...

Enough matches for a thousand forest fires.

She tore homes apart and made rivers rise.
Her anger startled no one...

Yet, I heard a voice at once
                          insistent...

Who cared what others thought?

Irene came up the coast—contender
of broken hearts .... Her whirling body
matched the spasticity of mine.
She understood chaos and the impossibility
of a tranquil life.

She was the woman of my dreams.

> *"The cabin in the Woods was made for happy people…*
> *who feel sad sometimes"*

So reads **Laureen Summers'** first published poem by a small magazine in 1968. With the feel of a haiku, it intended to express a gentle reconciliation with nature.

She began writing poetry in college to try to communicate this love of nature and the world around her. Her fascination with watching how people related to her, as well as to each other is reflected in many of her poems as well as an appreciation of nature and an attempt to face the struggle to understand herself as a woman with a disability. Learning to ride a bicycle, taking a balloon ride, walking across a monkey bridge, weaving wall hangings, hiking in the woods, and building a diverse group of friends and associates have challenged the assumptions and stereotypes that many have about people with physical disabilities.

Laureen was born with Cerebral Palsy in 1947. She began her life in New York and, after some years in Baltimore, moved with her family, to Puerto Rico when she was ten. She left after eight years of absorbing Puerto Rican culture and forming lasting friendships, to earn an A.A. degree in Liberal Arts at Cazenovia College in New York. She completed her B.A degree in 1971 at the College of the Potomac, in Washington, DC. She has taken additional coursework in Special Education and Teaching at the George Washington University.

Laureen moved to the Washington D.C. area in 1969 and became ensconced in the vibrant and alternative culture of DuPont Circle. Almost as soon as she settled, she joined the "Mass Transit" poetry group where many D.C. poets gathered over words and wine. It was also where she met Earl, her husband of 43 years.

She is Project Director of Entry Point!, an internship program for college students with disabilities at the American Association for the Advancement of Science. Since 1996, she has been involved with this program, which afforded summer opportunities to over 600 students, many of whom have become working scientists.

www.ingramcontent.com/pod-product-compliance
Lightning Source LLC
LaVergne TN
LVHW041506070426
835507LV00012B/1361